4801

BY

Anthony D. Williams Sr.

Dedication

To My Mother

Freedom

By

Tony

As a child, you gave me no freedom. You guarded my every move. I couldn't and didn't understand. I thought you were the meanest person on earth, yet I always wanted to be near you. Your words could make me tremble, but I never wanted you to leave me alone. As I grew older, you allowed me the freedom to laugh, learn, and cry- 'as long as your heart stays grounded, son.'

Then things changed. I could see it in your eyes. I heard the words, yet your eyes told a different story… a story this grown man couldn't understand. You said you were okay, and I believed you. You would never lie to mama. Now, the truth has come out. Well, as much as you cared to share, I feel like a child again. My heart ripped from my chest. A grown man broken. As I write these words, I cry. Remembering how stubborn you were. Those last few days of watching your body do what your spirit wouldn't… give up.

I knew you were suffering

I knew you were scared

I knew…

You would have never seen me cry like I'm crying now, Mama. Grown men aren't supposed to cry. Now I realize that freedom I foolishly wanted from you, you could not give. It's always been your nature to hold on. This would be your last day, your final place, when I realized what freedom really was…

Sitting in the back room as you lay in rest, I was alone and in my thoughts. Freedom was given. GOD intervened and freed us both. You from your physical pain and me from emotional. Some people cried; most were silent… I smiled, Mama — I am free.

About The Author

Anthony D. William Sr. grew up in Memphis, Tennessee, and has been part of law enforcement since 1993 (30 years). In 2015, he was a Lieutenant in the Memphis Police Department's Domestic Violence Unit. Among other DV cases, they also investigated elder abuse cases, and he got to see firsthand how horrendous those cases were. That's what inspired him to create his advocacy titled 'Teaching a Lion to Sing,' which has its own Facebook page under that title. This has also been an inspiration for creating the characters in this piece of literature. The author creates PSAs and publishes his own work on that Facebook page.

The book is a dedication to the author's mother, as he was very close to her, who has since passed away. She was, and still is, his biggest motivation.

ACT I

Scene 1:

Fade in.

Int. Bedroom-Day

Audio: Soft, melodious music

The camera pans a wall full of pictures, slowly taking in each and every frame. Some of the pictures are in black and white, while the rest in technicolor. It takes in several pictures of an old couple alone. One frame shows their wedding day, the couple looking into each other's eyes. The frame next to it shows them laughing at the camera. The camera moves to another frame where the woman is pregnant with a child. The camera then pans to the next set of frames, where the couple is playing with their young daughter. In the last frame, the young woman looks radiant, and the old man and woman standing next to her are smiling proudly. The last frame shows the young woman, along with her toddlers and the grandmother, all smiling at the camera.

Cut to

Ext. Inner City-Side Street View-Day

Audio: Intro music fades.

The camera freezes on an old house with a broken porch and faded paint. It zooms in, focusing on a window that is located on the side of the residence. It faces the neighbor's house, which is completely different from this one, with a well-kept yard and the house itself in good condition. An aerial shot of the neighborhood is shown, where the old house is the only unkempt house on the street. The camera gain pans back to the side window and zooms in till it shows an open, large plastic green garbage can located just outside the window. The garbage can is overflowing, and a large number of flies are buzzing around near the trashcan. Frame freezing on the lone window.

Cut to

The camera pans to the front door of the house, it's paint chipped and the number 4801 stenciled on it.

Scene 2:

Int. Bedroom-Day

The scene opens to a shabby, dark room. The sunlight pouring through the lone window is weak and barely lights up the space. The camera pans from the wall full of frames to a rickety four-poster bed. Right next to the bed is a small side table, with one leg broken. The furniture looks old and worn. The camera pans back to the bed where a frail African-American woman is lying, her whole body covered with sheets. She's lying facing the side table, where there are two picture frames showcasing her deceased daughter and husband at display. The camera shows one side of her face, where her lips are in a partial grimace, and a tear slips from the corner of her eye. She closes her eyes, a frown marring her forehead.

Cut

Scene 3:

Ext. Outdoor-Day

Audio: Rap music- Jorja Smith, 'Blue Lights'

An AMC Eagle Sedan, with blaring music, came rushing down the block and screeched to a halt right outside house 4801. The car was a 1982 model but in mint condition. The doors opened, and two young African-American boys, Ricky (17) and Jesse (19) got out of the car. They are wearing baggy jeans, baseball jerseys, and bandanas. They make it to the porch when the front door opens, and an 18-year-old black boy emerges. He's tall and thin, with tattoos covering his arms and neck. He smiles, and chest bumps both the guys.

JESSE

Yo, Tyler, today better be a good game, and I hope you've got enough alcohol for all of us. Last time, it was too much drama at ya place, dude!

                    TYLER

     Don't worry, man, I got the booze,
     food, and an effin' great game laid
     out for us. It's gonna be wild.

                                        Cut To

Scene 4:

Int. Lounge-Day

Audio: Kendrick Lamar 'DNA'

The music played on the stereo. Another
black guy, older than all of them, was
setting up the card table. Adam (21). He
fist-bumped all of them as they all settled
around the table, with a beer can taken
from the side table strewn with cold beer
cans and bags of chips.

                    ADAM

     Hey, fellas, I got some goodies. I
     want all of ya to try… they are the
     new thang.

                    JESSE

     It better not be that candy (crack)
     shit you raved about last time, did
     nothin' for me. I want hard stuff.

                    TYLER

     I ain't doing no purple (Ketamine)
     either. It messes me up, man.

                    ADAM

Relax, you sissies, don't get ya
panties in a twist. The stuff I got is
dope. Gentlemen, meet Dimitri, our new
friend. It's gonna take us soarin'.

Adam smiled as he produced a small bag of
powder that was clearly to be sniffed up.

                    RICKY

What it do? Can I try it?

                    ADAM

Nah, kid, I got the poppers for ya.
They'll get ya there for a short
period of time. That's all ya can take
for now. As for these bad babies,
Dimitri gives an intense high. It
makes ya float.

                    TYLER

Cool, but let's try this once we are
done with the game. I wanna play poker,
and this time, the stakes are high!

                    JESSE

Ya bet, man!

                    ADAM

Sure, let's play some card, fellas, but
hey, Tyler, you better have dough up
your ass. I'm not gonna play dry-ass
poker with ya if you don't have money.

                    TYLER

     I got money, bruh! The government's
     old age allowance cheque for Nonna
     just came in, and I had it cashed. So,
     your boy here is loaded.

                    RICKY

     Cool man, at least your grandmomma is
     of some use.

They all sniggered, Tyler laughing with
them.

                                        Cut To.

Scene 5:

Int- Kitchen-Day

Emma is washing the dishes in a dingy
kitchen, a small window showing an opening
into their unkempt backyard. The kitchen
area only has space for a stove, a fridge,
and a small cabinet. Emma puts the washed
dishes on the drying rack, then opens the
fridge and takes out the leftover pizza.
She plates it and heads out.

                                        Cut To

Int. Lounge-Day

Audio: Kendrick Lamar 'DNA'

The sound of blaring music and cigarette
smoke greets her as she enters the lounge.
She looks at the four boys sitting around

the table, playing poker, eating chips, and drinking beer. They are also smoking weed, and the smell clings to the air. She also sees the small power packets on the table and sighs. She knows her brother's friends will get high and crash at their place. This would be a cue for her to scoot and lock herself in her room.

                    JESSE

     Hello, baby doll, you look lovely in that sundress. Why don't ya come and say hi to us? How about play some poker.

                    TYLER

     Shut it and stop hittin' on ma sister. She's just fifteen, man.

                    RICKY

     Doesn't look like fifteen (mumbled)

                    TYLER

     What did ya say?

                    RICKY

     Nothin' man, chill!

                    ADAM

     RELAX, TYLER JESSE WAS FUCKIN' WITH YA. NOW, FOCUS ON THE GAME.

Tyler glared at Jesse and Ricky, then looked at Emma, who simply shrugged. She was used to this treatment. Her cinnamon-colored almond eyes, fuller lips, and curvaceous figure always drew unnecessary attention toward her. But since she barely left the house and had dropped out of high school, things weren't that bad, apart from the losers that her brother brought home.

She ignored the boys and continued eating the cold pizza. Her mind drifting.

Fade Out

Scene 6:

Fade back In

Ext. Outside-Day

Audio: Sound of laughter- Birds chirping

Emma (5 years old) is running in a playground. She is laughing, every few minutes looking back. Someone is chasing her, but the figure is hazy.

EMMA

(GIGGLING)

Come catch me, Momma…

MOTHER

I'm gonna get ya, baby girl.

EMMA

See, Momma, I run faster than Tyler.

Suddenly, Emma is about to stumble when the woman catches her and lifts her up. Her face not showing.

MOTHER

Gotcha, baby girl!

Emma squeals with joy, her mother's laughter ringing in.

Fade Out.

Scene 7

Fade In

Int. Lounge-Day

Audio: Rap song

ADAM

(SCRUNCHES NOSE)

What the fuck is that smell?

RICKY

Yeah, man, it stinks.

JESSE

Uh-oh, it must be your Nonna, man. She must have messed herself again. You gotta do somethin' about it, bruh. It kills the mood every time.

TYLER

Fuck! Emma, go see what she's done
now?

Emma, lost in her reverie, looks at him
startled.

EMMA

If your friends have issues, why don't
you go? Can't you see I'm eating?

TYLER

Don't ya test ma patience, woman. You
know you gotta take care of her, not
me. I pay the bills; you clean the
house.

EMMA

Huh… you don't pay the bills. You
cheated her of her welfare money as
well as her pension. You ass!

TYLER

Don't piss me off! Or I'll beat the
fucking hell out of you. Now, before I
really lose my temper, just go get her
cleaned up.

ADAM

Easy man, like ya said, she's just a
kid. She'll go, like always. No need
ta yell at her.

Adam motions her to go, and Emma glares at her brother, who's turned his back and is now snorting some Dmitri, completely oblivious to her. She looks at Adam and others in resignation. Her expression deflated and despondent.

Cut

ACT II

Scene 1

Fade in.

Int. Lounge-Day

Audio: Rap song

Emma (15) is standing in the middle of the lounge, looking deflated and angry. She takes in the scene, seeing the four boys playing poker, drinking beers, and joking around, completely ignoring her presence. She looks at her half-eaten pizza slice; her stomach grumbles, but the smell is now getting too much. She scrunches her nose and slowly turns toward the corridor.

Cut to

Int. Corridor-Day

Audio: Rap music fades

The camera tracks Emma as she runs down toward the far end of a dark corridor. She approaches the farthest room located in the back of their tiny residence. The door is stripped of paint, and the door knob is broken. She stops at the door, sighing heavily, her fists clenched. She looks at the door with trepidation and then flings it open.

Cut to

Scene 2:

Int-Lounge-Day

Audio: Rap music

The four boys are sitting around the table playing poker. The camera pans focus on the poker chips, then pans toward the strewn empty beer cans on the floor, along with chip wrappers and empty pizza boxes. The camera again pans toward the boys and focuses on Tyler (18). He takes the powder from the small bag and snorts it.

TYLER

Man, this stuff is lit!

JESSE (19)

Yeah dude… this shit…is hittin'

ADAM (21)

See, I told y'all! This new stuff will make us float… here Ricky, try these poppers… time for ya to get high, ma man!

Ricky catches a small yellow bottle and takes out some powder to snort it up. He inhales and puts the bottle aside, his body going lax and eyes glazing over almost a minute later.

RICKY

Fuck!

The three older boys laugh at Ricky, seeing him get high.

                                          Cut To

Scene 3:

                                          Fade In

Int-Bedroom-Day

Emma is standing on the threshold; the camera shows the room from her POV. The room is bathed in darkness, the window closed, the dustbin in the far corner of the room is full of trash and overspilling. There are soiled sheets bundled up in the far corner of the room. The camera cuts back to Emma as she enters the room and turns toward the wall full of pictures. She looks at the photo frames hanging from the wall. From one hand, she is pinching her nose, trying not to breath in the smell. She pauses in front of one photo frame. The camera pauses and zooms in on the picture, showing Emma as a child holding the hand of a woman who's her mother. She takes the frame off the wall and clutches it to her chest.

A loud wail escapes her mouth, and the camera zooms in on the sobbing girl as she falls to her knees and sobs.

                                          Fade out

Scene 4:

Fades back in

Ext: Outdoor-Evening

Audio: Rain and thunder

                    EMMA (5)

Don't go, momma… please don't leave
me.

                    MOTHER

Baby girl, your Nonna ain't well. I
need to get her medicine. Tyler, baby,
take your sister inside. I'll be
quick.

                    TYLER (8)

It's rainin' hard, Momma. Please don't
go…

                    MOTHER

Relax, baby. Nonna really needs the
meds. Now be a peach, and you both go
inside… I'll be back soon, babies.

                    EMMA

No, Momma no… I'm scared of thunder.
Please don't leave me alone, take me
with you.

MOTHER

Now, honey, don't be like this.
Besides, you're not alone. Nonna and
Tyler both are with you.

EMMA

No, I don't wanna be with 'em. I wanna
be with you!

MOTHER

Enough, hon. Now, Tyler, please take
your sister with ya, and no more
cryin', okay?

The children's mother hugs both of them and
then hoists Emma up, gives her another hug,
and kisses her on the cheek, brushing away
her tears. She puts her back down and then
motions them to go inside the house. They
back away and stand on the doorway as they
see their mother rushing toward her car,
getting in and driving away in the rain.

Fade Out

Scene 5

Fade in

Int-Indoor-Day

Audio: Fading sirens

Camera opens on Emma's crouched figure, her face
red with anger, tears streaming down her face.

EMMA

It's all your fault. You took her away from us… do ya hear me… you're responsible!

The camera pans toward the bed, where only soiled sheets are in view. Then pans back to Emma, who's hanging the picture frame back on the wall. Her face contorted with pain and misery. She moves toward the bed and goes and sits on the edge, looking at the sheets malevolently. She starts weeping again, covering her face with her hands.

Eventually, she stops and jumps up from the bed, picking up disinfectant from the edge of the bed that she had earlier placed there. There's fire in her eyes, and her face is tear-stained. The camera follows her as she rushes toward the window and forces it open, taking in the air from the outside, as there are no screens or bearers between herself, the stench, and the outside.

Cut To

Scene 6

Int-Kitchen-Day

Tyler is in the kitchen, getting more beer cans out of the fridge. Adam joins him, the camera showing a wide shot of the small dinghy room.

ADAM

Word on the street is that there's a
real market for Dimitri and poppers
when it comes to high school kids.

TYLER

Yeah… I heard oxy is no longer a go-to
for 'em.

ADAM

Ya know, white kids are suckers for
tryin' new things.

TYLER

That's true, man…

ADAM

So, what'd ya say? Shall we partner
up?

TYLER

Partner up for what?

ADAM

For selling this new shit, man!

TYLER

Dude, I ain't got the funds.

ADAM

You've got the old woman's monthly cheques.

TYLER

Yeah, but they ain't enough. We also
gotta spend some on her meds.

ADAM

C'mon, man, skipping a few meds ain't
gonna kill her. Besides, you can
double the money once we start
sellin'.

TYLER

I dunno, man. Lemme think 'bout it.

ADAM

Sure, but just lettin' ya know, I
already got Charlie after my ass for
putting in the money. But you like a
brother to me, so I gotta look out for
you first.

TYLER

Appreciate it, bro… I'll let ya know
soon.

The camera pans from Tyler's thoughtful
expressions to Adam's face, zooming on his
face, showing a calculating smile on his
face.

Cut To

Scene 7

Int-Bedroom-Day

The camera opens from the overflowing trash
can outside the window. It pans toward the
window and zooms in on Emma, whose eyes are
closed, and is taking deep breaths. She
slowly opens her eyes and then turns toward
the bed. The camera tracks her movement as
she comes nearer to the bed and takes in
the spoiled sheets and the disheveled bed.
The camera starts tracking the spoiled
white sheets fully stained from the foot of
the bed, tracking upward to the head, where
an old frail woman with curly greying hair,
sunken eyes, and sickly pallor is lying
down. Her face is tear-stained, her mouth
in a grimace. Her left eye twitches, and
she looks at Emma with helplessness. She
can't make a sound, and her body doesn't
move; it only slightly twitches as Emma
leans forward angrily. Her expression
scaring the older black woman.

                        EMMA

        All you do is make ma life more
        miserable than it already is. Your
        illness took away my momma. Now it'll
        take away mine slaving after you.

The camera pans from Emma back to her
grandmother as her facial expressions
change from fear to shame, another tear
rolling down her eyes as she looks away

from Emma. Her mouth was now a tight line
in misery.

Cut

ACT III

Scene 1

Fade in.

Ext-Neighbor house-Day

An African-American man steps out of a well-maintained house. It's painted white and also has a picket fence. The man seems to be taking out the trash. He moves toward his front yard, the camera following him. He takes the trash and dumps it in the trash can. Then, he turns around and stops to look at his neighbor's dilapidated home. The camera shows an AMC Eagle Sedan parked outside that house, then swivels back to show the man glaring at the car and shaking his head.

Cut To

Scene 2

Int-Bedroom-Day

The scene opens with Emma furiously snatching the sheets off of the old frail woman. The camera zooms in on the pained expressions of the old woman as she flinches when Emma takes off the sheet, and the woman is shown wearing a threadbare faded flannel nightgown, stained with dried blood, food stains as well as dried fecal matter. The woman's emaciated frame is quite visible, with her chest seemingly caved in. The woman's face is gaunt, and that's why her eyes bulge out more prominently.

The camera tracks Emma's movements as she hurriedly yanks another sheet out of bed. It is also stained with blood, urine, and fecal stains. As Emma further pulls away soiled sheets from underneath her grandmother, her body jerks every time. The woman flinching in pain.

Cut To

Scene 3

Fade in

Int-Bedroom-Day

Camera pans to a small shoebox kind of room, with faded pink paint on the walls. It pans to a disheveled small bed strewn with clothes, some pieces of cheap costume jewelry, and a few tattered books.

The camera zooms in on one of the books, which has a raunchy cover of a man schmoozing a scantily dressed woman. A hand picks up the book, and the camera tracks the movement of the hand, stopping on the face of its owner. Jesse looks at the book with a snigger, then moves toward a small purple dresser with a cracked mirror shoved against the wall in a corner. The dresser is cramped with items of makeup, more jewelry, and half-used bottles of deodorants and body sprays. There are polaroid pictures of Emma taped on one side of the mirror. Jesse peers at them, gliding a finger slowly through each photo. He then pauses at one picture, and the camera zooms in from his POV. The picture shows Emma dressed in a spaghetti strap summery dress, pouting at the camera.

                    JESSE (GROANS)

     Man…

                    TYLER (V.O.)

     Jesse, where ya at, man… why'd ya
     takin' so long.

Jesse twists his mouth in a grimace, then quickly retraces his steps out of Emma's bedroom, pausing at the threshold to give one last lingering look toward the room.

                                        Cut To.

Scene 4:

Int-Bedroom-Day

The camera opens with Emma pulling away the last of the linen from the bed, this time a little too hard. The woman's entire body jerks up, and her nightgown rides up, leaving the woman's legs and half of her thighs exposed. There are bed sores evident on her ravaged skin. Some old and some pretty new, with blood and puss oozing out of them.

The camera slowly tracks from the sores on her feet to the top part of her knees, and then her exposed arms where there's also a gash, showing that sometime in the past, the woman was injured with a sharp object, yet the wound didn't heal. The camera pans toward the soiled linen at Emma's feet, where she throws away the last of the linen sheet, which might have been once white but is now stained brown and crusty, with dark stain marks on it.

Emma scrunches her nose; she bends down to collect the pile of sheets from the floor and quickly rushes toward the open window. She tosses the sheets outside the window and into the large green trashcan outside the window.

Scene 3-A

Int-Lounge-Day

Audio: Rich Flex by Drake and 21Savage

Jesse enters the lounge, camera showing Tyler, Adam, and Ricky all sitting on the sunk-in sofa, watching a basketball game on the T.V., whilst eating pizza.

TYLER

What the hell were ya doin' in the loo for so long?

ADAM

Probably playin' with himself.

They all sniggered at him, and Jesse gave them all a finger.

JESSE

Fuck off y'all! Btw who won?

TYLER

I did, ma man! Your homie cleaned the house.

Jesse looked at Tyler with surprise and then looked at Adam questioningly, who simply smirked and winked at him.

JESSE

Wow! That's cool, man. Your first win against Adam. Must be somethin'

TYLER

Yeah, dude. Must be ma lucky day.

RICKY

Uhh, guys… do ya guys remember Perry Edwards? The fat ass that joined Antoine Richard's gang, running from Orange Mound?

ADAM

Yeah… isn't he your distant relative or somethin'? Heard he joined BGD (Black Gangster Disciples).

                    RICKY

Yeah… well, he got shot last night and
died. It was some gang-related
shooting. Dunno, Momma didn't tell us
a lot.

                    TYLER

Damn! He was cool. I liked him… used
to roll out cash to us whenever he was
in the neighborhood.

                    JESSE

Yeah! What a fuckin' waste.

                    RICKY

Hmm… Momma says BGD now wants Perry's
younger brother to jump in and join
them! They say Terry gonna go in
hiding. He ain't wanna be part of it.

                    JESSE

Smart kid! That's some shit I wanna
stay away from.

                    TYLER

I heard they pay real, good
though…like money wise, they take care
of ya.

                  ADAM (NODDED)

Real talk!

He looked thoughtful as he took a swig from his beer bottle.

Fade out

Scene 5

Fade in

Int-Bedroom-Day

The camera tracks Emma as she walks back and heads toward a small cupboard in the far corner of the room. She opens the cupboard. Takes out some faded white linens and comes back to the bed, dumping them on one side. She then picks up a disinfectant from the side table and begins to spray the entire bed area. Emma sprays everywhere, careless of the fact that the spray is hitting the open bed sores of her grandmother as well; it's going in her slightly open mouth. As the spray starts hitting the open sores, the grandmother's body starts shaking and flinching, her eyes tearing up as her breathing is becoming labored due to the stinging pain caused by the disinfectant as well as it's droplets going in her eyes and mouth, making breathing difficult for her. The woman twitches, and a silent sob wracks her body as she tries to establish eye contact with Emma to just stop, but Emma studiously avoids her and sprays more vigorously at the woman's wounds. It seems like she seems to be enjoying the other woman's misery. The camera pans to the older woman as Emma throws the clean linen over her grandmother's frail body. The scratchy fabric comes in contact with the sores, causing friction and further notching up the pain. Her face is a mask of agony.

Camera Freeze.

ACT IV

Scene 1

Fade In

Int-Bedroom-Evening

The old woman is propped up against the pillows, wearing a clean flannel gown. She seems to be in better health, although she's coughing every few minutes, and her eyes are teary. The camera pans from her face to the clean sheets and a quilt covering her legs. It swivels and slowly takes in the room that is clean, the bedside table devoid of any clutter. The paint on the walls seems fresh, and the photo frames are all neatly aligned on the wall. The curtain hanging on the window isn't threadbare but a nice gingham pattern.

                    EMMA'S MOTHER

You're awake; I was just coming to wake you up. Time for your medicine.

A young woman in her early thirties walks in, striding toward the side table, and opens the drawer. She takes out a medicine box.

                    EMMA'S MOTHER

Ma, you're out of this medication, and you can't miss a dose of it. Why didn't ya tell me?

                    GRANDMA (COUGHING)

You've been on your feet since
mornin', and it's crappy weather out
there... I could go without it for a
day.

The old woman is seized by another bout of
coughing, and she starts wheezing. Her
daughter immediately grabs a glass of water
from the nightstand and helps her mother
drink it, all the while rubbing her
mother's back in soothing circles.

                    EMMA'S MOTHER

No, Ma. You can't skip your
medication. Your coughing is getting
really bad, and your lungs can't take
the strain.

                    GRANDMA (COUGHING)

It's not that bad, don't worry. I'll
just have some soup, and that'll fix
me right up! I don't want you going
out in this wretched weather.

                    EMMA'S MOTHER

I can't stop worrying about you. In
the past couple of days, your health
has declined, and the doctor was very
strict about the instructions. I need
to go get the meds. I'll be quick.

                    GRANDMA

No honey… It looks like a storm is
raging outside. I don't want you to
go.

                  EMMA'S MOTHER

You know I can drive, Mama. Trust me,
I'll be careful. We can't skip a dose,
and you know it too…

                    GRANDMA

But-

                  EMMA'S MOTHER

No buts, Ma. Just take care of the
kids while I'm gone. I promise I'll be
quick. Let me get you settled so you
can keep a check on the kids.

The woman helps her mother out of the bed.
Both of them making their way toward the
door slowly.

                                   Fade Out

Scene 2

                                   Fade In

Int-Bedroom-Day

The old woman is now lying in her bed, her
face ravaged with time, ill health, and
neglect. She looks at the camera in

anguish, breaking the 4ᵗʰ wall. Tears stream down her face as her granddaughter jostles her body here and there, all the while cursing her fate.

                    EMMA

     I want out of this hell hole… I can't
     stand this no more… I'm too young for
     this shit.

The camera pans to Emma's furious expression as she yanks the last soiled sheet from the bed and throws it on top of the pile of other soiled sheets. She stoops down and grabs the pile, keeping her face averted from it, and quickly rushes toward the open window. The camera tracks her as she throws the pile of soiled sheets on top of the already overflowing large green trashcan.

She heaves drily as bile rises up in her throat. Eventually, she calms down and turns toward the room. A long shot of the disheveled room.

                                      Cut To

Scene 3

Ext-Backyard-Day

                                      Fade In

The camera opens to a manicured backyard, zooming in on the well-cut grass to a children's swing and a small tricycle lying on the ground. An African American man is raking fallen leaves to one side. He is Tyler and Emma's neighbor. He rakes the last of the leaves to one side and then takes the whole pile of it and puts it in a black garbage bag. As he ties the bag and looks up, he sees Emma throwing the soiled sheets. The camera shows from the man's POV as Emma turns her back toward him. The camera zooms in, partially showing the room - head shot of the old woman lying in the bed.

The camera swivels back to the man as he pauses, a look of concern evident on his face. He takes in the overflowing large trash can and the unkempt backyard of his neighbors. The man sighs, the camera tracking his viewpoint and closing in on Emma, who has turned to close the windows. She notices the man looking at the window; their eyes meet, and Emma pulls a face as she hurriedly closes the windows. The man looks worriedly at the closed window and shakes his head.

Fade Out

Scene 4

Fade In

Int-Bedroom-Day

Emma takes a deep breath, grabs an air freshener from the shelf, and sprays it liberally, trying to mask the smell. She looks toward the bed, then quickly tucks in the fresh sheets, which she had earlier thrown upon the old woman. Tucking the sheets tightly, she surveys the woman, ignoring her tears of pain. Turning on her heel, she dashes out of the room, closing the door loudly behind her.

The camera zooms in on the closed door, then panning toward the old woman, left with tightly bundled in the sheets, her teary eyes staring at the ceiling.

Cut

Scene 5

Fade In

Int-Lounge-Evening

Audio: Slow, melodious music

The camera opens up in a well-furnished lounge decorated in different tones of white and beige. The only splash of color comes from the paintings hung on the wall and the three ancestor masks painted in varying shades of ochre, hanging side by side on the main wall.

The neighbor is lounging on the sofa, looking at the T.V. screen but deep in thought. He looks outside the window toward the ramshackle neighboring house.

A svelte African-American woman enters the room and hands the man a glass of whiskey.

SHEILA (WIFE)

WHAT'S EATING YOU UP?

THOMAS (NEIGHBOR)

I'm worried about Mrs. Earl. Her grandchildren don't treat her right.

SHEILA

You're talking about the old woman living with her two grandkids next door, right?

THOMAS

Yeah.

SHEILA

Well, I've heard they are sponging off her money. And Mrs. Talbot told us that she tried seeing Mrs. Earl and was quite insistent, but her grandson barred her from coming back.

THOMAS

Hmm... I've seen the crowd that boy hangs with, and his younger sister is caring for the old woman. But her attitude is full of disdain. I've been mulling over it and have been watching them.

SHEILA

What have you seen?

THOMAS

That Mrs. Earl is not well. They are
mistreating her. I'm going to report
them for neglect and elder abuse.

SHEILA

Are you sure? What if you're wrong?

THOMAS

Then I'll apologize, but I'd rather
take my chances and get the
authorities to check in on her rather
than leave her to her own devices and
at their mercy.

The man states firmly, an implacable look
on his face.

Fade Out

Scene 6

Montage:

- Time-lapse of days changing - day into
  night.

- The old woman is shown wheezing and
  coughing, blood trickling from her
  mouth.

- Emma going about her business of
  cleaning, cooking, and watching T.V.

- Tyler getting drunk and hanging out with his friends outside the house.

Fade Out

Scene 7-A

Fade In

Int-Lounge-Bedroom-Day

Emma is cleaning the lounge. She sweeps the floor with a mop, then, on afterthought, moves toward the back of the house. The camera tracks her as she opens the door and enters her grandmother's room. From her POV, the camera moves toward the bed, where the old woman is lying with her eyes closed. Her pallor looks ashen.

Emma looks closely at her grandmother, then calls out to her.

                    EMMA

    Grandma… (beat) Grandma…

She calls her name loudly but doesn't get any response. So she shakes the older woman, noticing blood and puss oozing out of sores on her arms and shoulder. Looking closely, she sees dried blood crusted near one side of her grandmother's mouth.

                    EMMA

    Oh God… is she dead… Grandma, wake up!
    (loudly)

Emma bends forward and again shakes the older woman, who seems to be unresponsive. Panicked, Emma yells for Tyler.

Cut To

Scene 7-B

Fade In

Int-Lounge-Bedroom-Day

Tyler is drinking beer and watching something on the T.V. He has just come in and gotten settled on the sofa.

EMMA (V.O.)

Tyler… Tyler… somethin' happened to Grandma!

Tyler hears Emma shouting and quickly stands up, dashing toward the room. The camera tracks him as he rushes inside the room.

Cut To

Scene 8

Fade In

Int-Bedroom-Day

Emma is trying to check her grandmother's pulse, but her hands are shaking. Tyler rushes in, smacking the door against the wall loudly.

                    TYLER

Why are you shouting? What the hell's
wrong?

                    EMMA

She ain't responding... I tried
sprinkling water on her, but she
didn't move.

                    TYLER

Shit... was she like this yesterday too?

                    EMMA

Uhhh... don't know. I didn't check on
her the whole day yesterday.

                    TYLER

What do you mean? What about giving
her food or water.

                    EMMA

Day before yesterday, I just gave her
some water as she wasn't opening her
mouth, so I just forced some water
down her throat. She seemed okay, I
guess.

                    TYLER

Fuck Emma, you're supposed to check on
her every day. How many times have I
told you we can't let her die? She's
our money.

                    EMMA

I'm not your slave, Tyler… she stinks.
It's making me sick! I needed a break
too…

                    TYLER

Well, look what your break did… now
the old cow might be dead.

                    EMMA

Is she really?

Tyler moves and checks her pulse and
then puts two fingers against the old
woman's nostril, whose breathing is
shallow.

                    TYLER

She's breathing but barely.

                    EMMA

We gotta take her to the hospital.

                    TYLER

Are you fucking crazy? They're gonna
ask us all types of questions.

                    EMMA

Well, if we don't take her, she'll
die, and that would bring a whole lot
of trouble.

                    TYLER (SHOUTS)

    Shit, shit…

They hear a loud banging on the door, and
both the siblings freeze.

                                        Cut To

Scene 9

Ext-Outdoor-Day, Indoor-Day

Audio: Police Sirens, thriller music

Two squad cars are parked outside the
ramshackle house of the old lady. Two
police officers with their guns in hand
move toward the door and knock loudly. They
wait a couple of minutes but get no
response. They knock once again loudly.

                    TYLER (V.O.)

    Fuck! Shit, shit!

Hearing the loud voice, they look at the
backup and the main officer, who nods. The
two reach an understanding and, in unison,
kick the door open.

                    POLICEMEN (V.O)

    Police!

They yell as they enter the house, cocking
their guns, finding the lounge empty,
running straight into the corridor leading
to grandma's room, camera tracking them.

They enter the room and survey the situation, glaring at a bewildered Tyler, Emma standing behind him, shaking. One of the policemen looks at the unconscious woman; his nose scrunches at the stench and at the state of her. They see Tyler leaning toward Emma, whispering something. Both the men raise their guns.

POLICEMEN

Freeze, don't move!

Tyler raises his hands up in the air and nudges Emma to do the same, their expressions horrified.

Freeze

ACT V

Scene 1

Int-Bedroom-Day

Emma and Tyler stand in the middle of the room, their hands raised in the air as the policemen inch toward them with guns raised at them.

                    1ST POLICEMAN

Who are you?!

                    EMMA (STAMMERS)

Sh- sh- she is our grandmother.

                    2ND POLICEMAN

Where are your parents!?

                    TYLER

They're dead!

                    1ST POLICEMAN

So, she's your guardian, right?

One of the policemen inquired. Both siblings nodded.

                    2ND POLICEMAN

Who cares for her? How long has she been sick?

EMMA

I care for her; my brother looks after the house. I- uh- I don't know how long, but when I came in, she was already like this. I got too tired of caring for her, I was exhausted, got sick myself.

Emma lied to the police, saying exactly what Tyler had told her to say the minute they'd heard sirens and loud banging.

Fade out

Scene 2

Fade In

Int-Bedroom-Day

Audio: Police sirens

Tyler angrily kicked the bed as he heard sirens on the street.

TYLER

Shit, shit! Emma, listen to me. You gotta cover for me!

EMMA

What do you mean, cover ya?

TYLER

Answer their questions and tell 'em you're taking care of her; you're tired sick, so it made it hard for you to look after her.

                         EMMA

     So, you want me to take all the blame?
     Say it's all my fault?

                         TYLER

     It is your fault, dammit! You should
     have paid attention. Now we don't have
     time for a fucking blame game. Just do
     as I say, answer the fucking questions
     and ask them to call paramedics,
     that's it. If you don't do it, they'll
     throw both of us in jail. Is that what
     ya want?

                         EMMA

     No! but…

They hear a loud crash and then heavy
footsteps, and both of them look scared.

                                        Fade Out

Scene 3

Int-Bedroom-Day

The policemen put their guns in the
holster, one of them once again going to
check on the old woman. From his POV, the
camera showed the passed-out frail woman,
with blood and vomit crusted near her
mouth. Her shallow breathing raising the
sheet covering her lightly.

EMMA

We were just gonna call an ambulance
when y'all came. Grandma needs to be
taken to the hospital.

Emma explained, wringing her hands.

2ND POLICEMEN

Hmmm...

1ST POLICEMEN

The kid's right; we need to call in
paramedics. I'll call it in.

He stepped out of the room, the other
officer kept a wary eye on both Emma and
Tyler.

Cut To.

Scene 4

Montage

- An ambulance arriving, and paramedics
  jumping out of it and heading into the
  house.

- The neighbors who reported the neglect
  standing on their porch, watching
  everything unfold.

- Paramedics entering the old woman's
  room and immediately hooking her to an
  IV drip and wiping her mouth, then

lifting her from the bed and putting her on a gurney.

- In the mayhem, Tyler is slipping away.

- The old woman being taken out of the house, strapped to a gurney, and being lifted in the ambulance.

- Emma being helped inside the ambulance to sit with her grandma.

- Day transitions into evening.

Scene 5

Fade In

Int-Hospital-Evening

Two E.R. nurses are rushing the gurney to which Emma's grandma is strapped toward the E.R. One of the paramedics is debriefing them, whereas one nurse is holding the oxygen mask over the old woman's face.

PARAMEDIC

Patient is 75 years old, named Mrs. Earl, suffering from atrophic arthritis. A stroke in the past has left her partially paralyzed. She is suffering from malnutrition, infected wounds, and extreme dehydration, and she has lost a lot of bodily fluid. We fear a stroke if immediate care isn't given.

The E.R. nurses nodded, one looking behind her to look at Emma, who was trailing

behind with police officers in tow. The
camera panned from Emma back to the grandma
being rushed into the ICU.

                    NURSE

     Page Dr. Richmond, the patient is
     critical and also call social
     services.

The camera tracked as the gurney was pushed
into a huge room, the doors shutting
behind. Leaving Emma behind with the
officer. Emma sat on one of the seats, her
shoulders hunched as she started sobbing.

                                  Cut To.

Scene 6

Int-Hospital-corridor

                 DR. RICHARDSON

     Is there any adult with you, or are
     you alone here?

                    EMMA

     Uhhh… my older brother is on the way,
     and the police officer just left.

                 DR. RICHARDSON

     Then I'll wait for your brother to
     discuss your grandmother's condition.
     She's out of danger but needs
     monitoring, so we're shifting her to a
     room.

Emma nodded, her expressions stricken with worry as she looked at the hospital exit longingly.

Cut To

Scene 7

Fade In

Int-Hospital room-night

Audio: Beep of monitors

The frame opens to a beeping monitor, panning to the figure lying on the hospital bed, covered with blankets. Emma's grandmother's hands are bandaged, and so is most of her face, which is covered with a mask and intravenous IV drips attached to both her hands. The camera then pans toward a corner of the room, where Emma is awkwardly dozing off on a chair. Her head lolling to one side.

A door opens, and Tyler slips in. He looks at the sleeping Emma, then slowly walks toward the bed. He looks at his grandmother in anger, mouth grimacing.

                    EMMA

     Ty?

                    TYLER

     Hey.

                    EMMA

Where did you go? The doctor and
officers asked me so many questions.

                    TYLER

I just needed to collect ma thoughts and
figure out how to clean up this mess.

                    EMMA

Yeah right! Anyway, doc's been asking
for ya.

                    TYLER

We gotta get out of here quick.

                    EMMA

We can't leave her behind.

Emma looked at her grandmother, a guilty
expression on her face.

                    TYLER

Of course not. We need to take her home.

                    DR. RICHARDSON

Not yet, young man. Your grandmother
isn't well and extremely malnourished.
We've stopped the spread of infection
by treating her wounds, but we would
like to admit her into a long-term
care facility to give her the full
treatment she needs.

                    TYLER

Thank you, Doctor, but I think we
wanna opt out of that option.

                DR. RICHARDSON

Trust me, your grandmother needs
constant vigilance and care, and she
would be comfortable in the facility.
You both are too young to care for her
like that.

                    TYLER

I understand, but I insist. Please
just treat her for now, and we'll take
care of the rest. We'll be more
vigilant.

                DR. RICHARDSON

It's a huge responsibility, are you
sure?

                    TYLER

Yeah. So, any idea when we can take
her home?

                DR. RICHARDSON

In a couple of days.

Dr. Richardson then turned to look at
his patient. After the checkup, he
gave both of them a long look before
walking out.

EMMA

You know we can't care for her. It's
too much; why don't ya agree to long-
term care?

TYLER

Because the care facility would be
entitled to her money if she entered
into long-term care. And I ain't lettin'
anyone get their hands on our money.

EMMA

Look at her. She almost died. I can't
keep on caring for her; it's too much.

TYLER

You don't have a fucking choice. She
can't die. You gotta look after her
and keep her alive.

EMMA (DEFIANTLY)

Or what?

TYLER (MENACINGLY)

Oh, you don't wanna know, sis. Trust
me!

After threatening her, Tyler glares at his
sister and slams the door behind him,
exiting the room. Emma sits defeatedly back
in the chair.

Cut To.

Scene 8

Montage

- Transitioning of day into night.

- Emma aimlessly wandering the hospital corridors, a nurse observing her.

- Tyler sneaking into the hospital, stealing fruit or some food items, even medical stuff from trolleys, to pawn things.

- Grandma being looked after by the hospital staff.

- A nurse wheeling grandma on the wheelchair outside the hospital, Tyler and Emma standing behind.

Fade Out

Scene 9

Int-Hospital

Dr. Richardson is sitting in a small room behind a small desk. Papers and files are strewn on the table, the camera pans to the wall where the doctor's various degrees have been framed and are on display. Few of the frames show him shaking hands with some influential people.

DR. RICHARDSON

I hope you've reviewed the case I
referred to you.

The camera swivels from Dr. Richardson to a
thin man sitting opposite him. His
expression taught and spectacled eyes
reviewing some papers that were in his
hand. He was the head of the hospital's
social service department.

MR. WATSON

I did, Doctor, and since there's
already a report filed for elder
abuse, you're right. A case worker
needs to be assigned to Mrs. Earl. The
kid looking after her is a juvenile,
and the older boy is still a teenager.

DR. RICHARDSON

Hmm… that boy was a slippery one. He
was adamant on taking the old woman
away. The three days she was here, he
kept on insisting to immediately
release her. I'm worried that she'll
be subjected to neglect once again if
we don't keep a check.

MR. WATSON

Agreed, we did assign someone to
observe those kids while they are
here, albeit discreetly. And based on
that, I've already decided to assign

the case to one social worker who's
good at this.

                    DR. RICHARDSON

Thank you. It will be a relief to know
someone is checking up on the poor old
woman.

A thoughtful expression is visible on the
doctor's face as Mr. Watson stands up and
shakes hands with him before exiting the
room.

                                    Freeze

ACT VI

Scene 1

Fade In

Ext-Hospital-Day

The camera opens to an orderly pushing an old woman in a wheelchair. The camera zooms in, and it is revealed that it is Emma's grandma, looking weak and frail. Emma and Tyler are trailing behind. The orderly stops outside an ambulance and puts the wheelchair on the ramp. After loading her in, Tyler and Emma also jump in the ambulance as they both are riding along with the patient.

The ambulance door closes, and the camera pans from closed doors to the hospital entrance, where Dr. Richardson and Mr. Watson are looking at the ambulance driving away.

Cut To

Scene 2

Ext-4801 House-Day

Tyler is now wheeling his grandmother inside the house, and Emma follows him. As they step in and the orderly follows, Tyler tries shutting the door on him.

TYLER

We can take it from here

ORDERLY

I have to settle her in. Let me do my
job, man.

Tyler makes a face as Emma leads the man to
her grandmother's room. The orderly takes
in the shabby surroundings and then
grimaces as he sees the disheveled state of
the room. He refrains from saying anything
and quickly removes the spoiled sheets from
the bed and asks Emma to put them in a
garbage bag. Then he takes out clean sheets
from his own medical bag, makes the bed,
and, with Tyler's help, carries the old
woman to the bed and lays her down. After
administering a sedative, he instructs Emma
to keep checking up on her every few hours,
then gives the woman a last look as he
heads out. The camera tracks his movement
and then pans to the old woman, who has
some color on her face but still looks ill,
and slowly, her eyes start drooping.

Fade Out

Scene 3

Int-Lounge-Night

Tyler is playing a card game with his
friends, all of them drinking. Emma comes
into the lounge.

EMMA

Tyler… grandma needs her medicines.
She's getting sick again. She just
threw up. It's been two days since
I've been telling you to get em'.

TYLER

I don't have time. Just clean her up.

EMMA

I did, but she ain't getting better.
We have to give her the meds!

TYLER

We'll see now. Get the fuck on! and
let us play in peace.

Tyler's two friends snicker at Emma. She
quickly turns around and leaves the room.
The camera tracks her to her grandmother's
room, where the old woman is lying on the
bed. Her frail body is twitching from time
to time, and drool escapes from one side of
her mouth. Tears of pain stream down her
face.

Cut To.

Scene 4

Ext-Street-Day

A middle-aged woman is sitting in a car,
fidgeting with her purse strap, as she
reviews a file in her lap. She looks up,

and the camera tracks her vision to the only dilapidated house on the street. She checks the I.D. card she's wearing around her neck, which shows she's a social worker appointed by the state. Gingerly, she gets out of the car and makes her way toward the run-down porch. The camera tracks her from behind as she knocks on the door of house 4801. While she waits, she wrinkles her nose as if she has smelled something bad in the air.

SOCIAL WORKER (V.O)

It smells like marijuana.

She waits a few minutes, then once again loudly knocks on the door, and after a beat, the door slowly creaks open. From her POV, she sees a young man in his late teens open the door and eyes her warily.

TYLER

Who the hell are you?

SOCIAL WORKER

Hi, I'm the social worker assigned to your grandmother. If you could let me in? I'd like to check on her.

TYLER

I know nothing about this social worker crap, lady. Can't let a stranger in ma house.

He tries to shut the door, but she stops him.

                    SOCIAL WORKER

     Here, this is my card, and you can
     check with the hospital. But I would
     really like to come in and just check
     how your grandmother is doing.

Tyler spares a glance at the card in her
hand, then threateningly steps toward her.

                        TYLER

     Listen, lady. My grandmother is just
     fine, and I don't care who you are.
     So, you can go back to your hospital
     and tell 'em you did your job and the
     old woman is fine. Bye!

Tyler steps back and shuts the door in her
face, making the woman jump with nerves.
For a minute, she had thought that he would
shove her. She looks around as she steps
off the porch. The camera tracks her going
around the house and looking through the
windows.

                                        Cut

Scene 5

Int-Lounge

Audio: Rap music

Tyler is smoking a joint, blowing smoke in circles; he's half lying, half sitting on the sofa enjoying the music, when he hears loud knocking. He tries to ignore it, but the banging goes louder.

                    TYLER

     What the fuck is wrong with this woman…
     gotta give her a piece of my mind.

He stalked toward the door and aggressively opened it. Looking angrily at the person knocking on the door. From his POV, he is stunned to see a policeman standing instead and the social worker sitting in her car. His eyes are bloodshot as he realizes that the officer can smell marijuana.

                    TYLER

     Uhh… officer, is there a problem.

                    POLICEMAN

     Yes, now kindly step away and let the
     lady do her job. Failure to do so will
     be treated as hampering legal procedure.

The Policeman warns him and gestures for the social worker to step outside the car and come inside the house. Tyler glares at the woman but doesn't say anything, letting her pass. He's smart enough to know not to mess with the police. Besides, he thought if he cooperated, he would get out of trouble.

                                   Intercut

The Policeman and social worker stand in the lounge, looking around and taking in the joint on the small table along with empty bottles strewn around. They move ahead along the corridor after asking Tyler to show his grandmother's room. The camera pans from the trio to Emma, who steps out of her room with bleary eyes. Tyler motions for her to remain quiet.

Cut To.

Scene 6

Int-Room-Day

The camera opens with the old woman lying in her bed, her sheets dirty with blood and fecal matter. As the social worker steps in and takes in everything, she grimaces, taking out a handkerchief to cover her nose.

POLICEMAN

Jesus.

The Policeman steps forward and cuffs Tyler.

POLICEMAN

You have a right to remain silent.

TYLER

What did I do?

POLICEMAN

You're being charged with abuse.

He then proceeds to cuff Emma, who has
started sobbing.

SOCIAL WORKER

Officer stops. You can't arrest this
girl. She's just fifteen, which makes
her a juvenile. She can't stand trial.
She needs to go into juvenile
detention.

The social worker explains this to the
officer, who nods, then calls back up to
pick Emma up. The social worker goes to her
and offers her a handkerchief, shaking her
head disappointedly at the young girl. The
officer then escorts both the siblings out
of the room.

Cut To

Scene 7

Int-Juvenile Detention Center

Emma is sitting in a room with two girls.
She is sobbing, her arms wrapped around her
knees, as she rocks back and forth, trying
to stop herself from screaming.

Intercut

Scene 7-A

Int-Jail Cell-Night

Tyler is lying on a stone slab in the far corner of a jail. There is a huge man sitting on the opposite side, glaring at him with hostility.

Intercut

Scene 7-B

Int- Home for the Aged

Emma's grandmother is lying on a small bed in a spartan room at an old age home facility. A nurse comes in, props her up against the pillows, and makes her drink some juice. She then feeds her some pudding and gives her some medicines. She then wipes the old woman's face, who looks better, her hands and feet bandaged. The grandmother looks well now that she is being properly taken care of.

Freeze

ACT VII

Scene 1

Fade In

Ext-Day-Building

A young woman in her late twenties strolls through the shops, wandering aimlessly, killing time. Her auburn hair shining in the glistening sun. The camera tracks her as she strolls past a shop, pausing to check her appearance in the mirrored window. She smooths the creases from her navy-blue pantsuit, straightening her ponytail and readjusting her sunglasses, hiding her sharp hazel eyes as well as protecting her honey-golden skin from the relentless sun. Satisfied with her appearance, she continues strolling. The camera takes a wide shot of a strip mall area, where passersby are strolling past various stores, some going in and some out.

The camera zooms in on the woman now talking on her phone.

MELISSA

Yes, you've reached Ms. Jimenez. How may I help you?

PERSON ON PHONE (V.O)

Well, prosecutor, we need to see you for a case. Is it possible if you could meet us early tomorrow at the address I'm texting you?

MELISSA

Of course, send me the details of the
case by email too. Yes, see you
tomorrow.

Melissa ends the call, her eyes following
upon a children's store, and her expression
softens. The camera tracks her gaze to the
shop.

Cut To.

Scene 1-A

The camera tracks Melissa as she scans
aisles of baby clothing. Pausing here and
there to look at newborn babies' toys and
essentials. Involuntarily, her hand goes to
her stomach, pauses, and stays there for a
second. She smiles, having just entered her
second trimester of pregnancy, although she
isn't showing yet.

SALE ASSISTANT

Hola puedo ayudar? (Hello can I help?)

Melissa turns to look around at the young
Hispanic girl, who must have figured out
Melissa's heritage too.

MELISSA

No gracias.

Melissa proceeds to look at a pair of small
booties, and the sales assistant exits. The

camera pans back to Melissa, who has picked up the booties and determinedly moves toward the checkout counter.

Cut.

Scene 2

Int-Home for the Aged-Day

The grandmother is sitting on a recliner, looking outside the window that opens into a large garden where other residents of the house are walking or sitting on the benches. The old woman is wearing a clean cotton long-sleeved gown and woven slides, her face no longer gaunt and haggard. Instead, she seems to be in much better health. The camera pans the small room, zooming in on a vase of fresh flowers.

INTERCUT

A nurse walked carrying a tray of food along a wide corridor. The camera tracks her as she slips a keycard out of her pants pocket and swipes it, opening the door.

Intercut

NURSE

Good morning, Mrs. Earl. How are you this morning?

The nurse steps forward and pulls up a small table in front of the old woman, setting the food tray on it.

                    GRANDMOTHER

     Good mornin'.

The old woman chokes the words out, her mouth twisting lopsidedly as she speaks. In the weeks that she has been at the old age house, her progress has been rather good, and despite her physical limitations, she has been able to speak small words and even take assisted walks for a few minutes out in the garden.

                      NURSE

     Great, let's get you some breakfast,
     then I'll get you changed and settled
     in bed. Oh, and also, we'll be having
     some visitors for you this afternoon.

The grandmother perks up and gestures to ask if the visitors are her grandchildren. She stutters a couple of times.

                    GRANDMOTHER

     Ttttyy…eh eh emmaaaaa…

The nurse shakes her head, and the old woman sags back in her seat. The nurse looks at her sadly, proceeding to place the napkin on her lap and tucking it under her collar. The camera pans from the nurse spooning the porridge and feeding the grandmother to the window overlooking the garden, zooming in on a large tree.

Cut

Scene 3

Int-Juvenile Detention Center-Day

Emma sits in a small classroom where an older woman is teaching girls her age some handcrafting. The camera pans the small rectangular room with bare walls, carpeted floor, small round tables, and chairs strewn around, with a large functional cupboard bolted to the floor, holding supplies for arts and crafts. Emma sits holding a small stitching kit, a large piece of fabric in her lap, for her to cut. Emma sighs and listens to the teacher's instructions. Her gaze strays back longingly to the barred window on the other side of the room.

                    TEACHER

> After you've made the required cut, please put away the remaining fabric in the basket over there and also put back your supplies too. You have your chores for the day in about ten minutes.

The girls start grumbling about the impending chores, but Emma simply stands up and slowly starts stowing the stuff away. She knows there is no point in objecting to anything. Every day is the same in these walls. A tear slides down her eye, and she quickly wipes it.

Cut

Scene 4

Int-Social Services-Day

The camera opens to a small room, spartanly furnished, the desk cluttered with a pile of files. The middle-aged social worker sits rocking in her chair as she goes over a file. She looks up nervously at the prosecutor sitting opposite her. The calm energy of Melissa Jimenez further flusters her.

MELISSA

It's a solid enough case. I had my assistant go around the neighborhood to question the neighbors, and the testimonials we got didn't look promising at all.

SOCIAL WORKER

Yes, I can see that in the charge sheet. I'm just worried if we should press charges against the young girl. She's a juvenile, only fifteen years old.

MELISSA

A fifteen-year-old who showed grievous negligence toward her own grandmother.

> Anyway, I phoned the old age home and
> made an appointment to see Mrs. Earl
> in about an hour. Let's grab some
> lunch before heading there.

The social worker nods, a little awed to
see the energy of the young women.

Cut To

Scene 5

Int-Home for the Aged-Afternoon

Audio: Light, harmonious music.

The camera takes a wide shot of a reception
area, where a young receptionist is typing
something on her computer. On the couch
opposite her, two elderly women sit,
watching a comedy show on the small T.V.
mounted on the wall. The camera tracks from
the reception area to the two women
stepping into the foyer, walking
purposefully toward the reception area.

Intercut

The grandmother is sleeping in her bed, her
mouth lax. The door opens, and the social
worker, nurse, and Melissa walk into the
room. Seeing her sleeping, the nurse
gestures to them to remain quiet. The women
nod and, with mutual agreement, start
inspecting the room. Checking for any
anomalies or mistakes by the place itself.
Melissa then picks up the medical chart and

surveys it. Satisfied, she looks intently at the sleeping woman, then turns to leave, the camera zooming in on the sleeping old woman.

Cut To

Scene 6

Montage:

- Tyler is wearing orange overalls, sitting in a prison cell, his face haggard from drug withdrawal. Shaking compulsively.

- Emma, working around the juvenile facility.

- Grandmother, walking in the hospital corridor with the aid of a walker. A physiotherapist helping her.

- Melissa and the social worker are looking at the old woman sitting in a wheelchair, enjoying the sun in the garden, and getting the status of her progress from the nurse.

- Melissa, sitting with the old woman in her room, showing her prosecutor's card to her and then taking the old woman's hand in hers in a reassuring gesture.

Cut

Scene 7

Int-Home for the aged-Evening

The camera tracks Malissa walking purposefully toward Mrs. Earl's room, the social worker trailing behind. Melissa's foot gets caught, and she's about to stumble, but the social worker quickly grabs her by the arm and helps her regain balance. Melissa's hand goes to her unseen baby bump to reassure herself.

SOCIAL WORKER

Are you alright?

MELISSA

Yes, I'm fine. Thank you. Please make sure Mrs. Earl signs the charges we're pressing on her grandchildren. And also, the papers for long-term care.

The social worker takes a deep breath as Melissa moves forward, the camera focusing on the social worker's expression.

Cut To.

Scene 8

Int- Home for the aged - Evening

The grandmother is lying in bed, propped against the pillows. She seems a little feverish. Melissa and the social worker enter the room with files in their hands.

MELISSA

Hello, Mrs. Earl. Hope you're doing well today. We just popped in to get some formalities done.

SOCIAL WORKER

Oh, yes, we just wanted to let you know that we're doing our very best to get a good outcome for your case.

The camera pans from the woman standing in the room to the nurse standing in the far corner, observing everything. The camera swivels to the grandmother, who was once again trying to speak and was stuttering. She beckoned the two women forward, and both went to her, leaning toward her to hear what she was trying to say.

GRANDMOTHER (WHISPERS)

P- p- please let m- m- my family be.

The old woman takes a deep breath, then, with effort, implores.

GRANDMOTHER

Please let me go home.

The camera focuses on her imploring expressions, then swivels to the prosecutor, looking unfazed, although the middle-aged social worker frowns and looks perplexed.

Freeze

ACT VIII

Scene 1

Fade In

Int-Prosecutor Office-Day

The camera opens into a small room with a large oak desk in the middle of the room. It pans from the bare walls to the spartan furnishing, swiveling back to Melissa sitting in a high-backed chair, sipping mint tea as she surveys some papers in front of her. Across her, the social worker is also busy perusing some legal documents, a frown on her face.

SOCIAL WORKER

So, we got a date for the hearing.

MELISSA

Yes, finally!

SOCIAL WORKER

Have you given another reconsideration to what Mrs. Earl wished for?

MELISSA

There's nothing to reconsider. She was just being emotional and sensitive. Classic case of Stockholm syndrome; trying to love and protect your captor. Her love for those grandchildren of hers is nothing but trauma bonding.

                    SOCIAL WORKER

You can't really say that. Sure, the
children have been despicable toward
her, but I'm sure her love for them is
genuine.

                      MELISSA

There's no doubt her love for them is
genuine, but that doesn't change
anything. Her grandchildren are both
complicit in elder abuse. Her trying
to protect them from getting punished
doesn't absolve them of their crime.

                    SOCIAL WORKER

Still, I think we should at least try
to get a pardon or reduced sentence
for the younger girl. It's only fair.

                      MELISSA

No, it's not! If you do something wrong,
you should be punished for it. Going
easy on them only means enabling them.

The firm set of Melissa's mouth made the
social worker bite her lip, and she shook
her head as she once again started going
through the papers in front of her. The
camera panned from her pinched expressions
to Melissa's implacable one as she leaned
backward in her chair, absently stroking
her belly shrouded in a multicolored cape.

                                        Cut

Scene 2:

Int-Juvenile Centre-Day

The camera opens to a large hall where some teenagers are busy doing chores. Two girls are wiping the large windows overlooking the garden. A boy and a girl are polishing the brass furniture. The camera pans from them to a lone girl on the far side of the roomer, sweeping the floor. The camera tracks her movements as she shuffles around with her mop and bucket of water. An officer enters the room and purposefully walks toward her. On reaching her, he hands her an official letter, the camera focuses on her shaking hands.

Cut

Scene 3:

Montage

- The old woman is sitting in an armchair in the care-home. Her face is masked with grave concern. She looks outside the window, tears streaming down her face.

- The social worker climbs the courthouse steps, pausing to catch her breath, when a squad car stops, and Emma is led out of it. The camera pans from Emma's downcast expressions to the social worker's apprehensive one.

- Tyler is led through the corridor of the courthouse. His face looks gaunt, and his thin frame shakes as he shuffles toward the court room.

Cut

Scene 4:

Int-Courtroom

Camera opens up in the middle of the courtroom, where both the prosecution and defense are preparing their opening statements. The camera slowly starts tracking the room from the rear door from where the judge enters and takes his seat.

JUDGE

Prosecution proceeds with the opening statement.

Melissa steps forward, wearing a maroon blazer and pants. The blazer fitting snugly over her protruding belly, as she has started showing.

MELISSA

Your honor, we are here to discuss the case of Earl Vs Earl. A case of gross negligence and elder abuse.

JUDGE

I see here that one of the accused is a juvenile?

                    MELISSA

Yes, your honor. Ms. Emma Earl is a
juvenile, Mrs. Earl's granddaughter.

                     JUDGE

Kindly continue with your opening
statement.

                    MELISSA

Thank you. The case is pretty simple.
Mr. Tyler Earl and Ms. Emma Earl, both
residents of house 4801, have been
complicit in being negligent toward
their ailing grandmother to the point
of the old woman being hospitalized
once and then the social worker having
to call the authorities to intervene
on her behalf. I've also submitted her
medical records along with her
physician's recommendations and
concerns regarding her care.

                     JUDGE

And Mrs. Earl is in a care home for
the elders, I presume?

                    MELISSA

Yes, your Honor.

                     JUDGE

Any other remarks before I call the
defense to make their statement?

                    MELISSA

    No, your honor, that would be all.

The camera tracks Melissa's movements as she turns on her heels, takes her seat, and looks at the defense lawyer making his statement. The camera then pans to a forlorn-looking Emma and an angry Tyler sitting in the backseats of the wooden benches.

                                        Cut

Scene 5

Int-Care home for elders

The scene opens with the nurse trying to feed soup to the grandmother, but she refuses to eat it as she looks agitated. Her eyes keep darting to the door as if expecting some kind of news. The camera zooms in on her quivering lips and shaking hands.

                    NURSE

    What's the matter today, Mrs. Earl?
    You look quite worried.

                    MRS. EARL

    Emmm… Ttyy… wh wh..

The old woman stutters, gesturing to ask about her grandchildren, and the nurse understands her nods.

NURSE

I'm sure they are fine. You just relax
and not worry about 'em. Right now, we
need to focus on your health. Now
please have some soup.

The nurse once again raises the spoon to
her lips and cajole the old woman to take
some sips. Liquid trickles out from one
side of her mouth, which the nurse dabs
with a napkin. The camera focuses in on a
tear escaping from the old woman's eye.

Cut

Scene 6

Int-Court room

Melissa is standing in front of the judge,
the social worker standing beside her,
giving her testimony to the judge. Each
time she falters or sends a furtive glance
at Tyler and Emma, the camera tracks her
movement. Melissa sees her looking back at
them and nudges her to focus on the judge.

MELISSA

Please explain how Mr. Tyler Earl
always tried to intimidate you when
you visited the ailing Mrs. Earl.

                    SOCIAL WORKER

Oh yes, your honor. It's just that Mr.
Tyler was a little stand offish and
impolite on my visitations.

                        JUDGE

And did he try to disrupt your
visitations in any shape or form?

                    SOCIAL WORKER

Uhh.. yes, sir.

                       MELISSA

And what happened the last time when
you had to call the cops to the house?

The Social Worker hesitated and then
started narrating the events, the camera
panning to Emma, who visibly flinched at
the statement, and then pans toward Tyler,
who's looking menacingly at the Social
Worker. The camera tracks to the Social
Worker; her eyes meet Tyler's, and she
visibly gulps before averting her gaze. The
camera swivels to Tyler and freezes on his
menacing scowl.

                                   Fade Out

Scene 7

Montage

    - The cops who were called on the scene

by the Social Worker are called to the witness stand.

- Melissa also shows the neighbor's testimonials to the court.

- Tyler is fidgeting in his seat, whereas Emma is silently crying.

- Both Melisa and the defense attorney are giving their closing statements.

- Emma is sobbing while the statements are being given, and her lips curl in disgust on hearing her grandmother's name since she still blames her for her mother's death.

- Melissa looks at crying Emma with a thoughtful expression, absently rubbing her stomach.

                                                    Cut

Scene 8:

Int-Court room

Melissa, the defense attorney, and the social worker stand in front of the judge, waiting for the verdict. Both the prosecutor and defense attorney have an expectant look on their face.

JUDGE

Considering all witness testimonials, there's no doubt it is a case of elder abuse, and the accused are responsible. However, I believe that before I give my final verdict, I would like to ask both the prosecutor and the social worker to give their recommendations on how we should proceed.

DEFENSE ATTORNEY

But your Honor…

The judge raises his hand and silences the protesting attorney, who frowns and then takes his seat. The camera pans to Melissa as she smiles with confidence.

SOCIAL WORKER

I uhhh… I don't know your honor… but…

The social worker falters as she is in unchartered territory. She looks at Melissa, who seems to be deep in thought, her hand on her baby bump, a tender expression on her face. The Social Worker looks at Melissa with a knowing look.

The camera tracks Melissa's movements as she rubs circles on her stomach bump in a soothing motion and starts crying.

JUDGE

Are you alright?

MELISSA

Yes, your Honor. Please give me a
minute.

She turns around, dabs her eyes, and looks
at Tyler and Emma, then recalls what Mrs.
Earl said while still touching her stomach.

Fade Out

Scene 9

Flashback

Int: Nursing Home for Elders-Day

- Melissa and the Social Worker are
  standing near the bed. Mrs. Earl is
  crying and touching her stomach. She
  beckons Melissa forward, and when she
  leans in, the old woman whispers
  something to her.

Fade Out

Scene 8-A

Fade In

Int-Courtroom-day

Melissa is standing in the middle of the
room, her gaze unfocused. She takes a deep
breath and pats her rounded stomach before
resuming her speech. The camera pans to the
judge.

MELISSA

Until coming to the court and compiling this case, I was sure that the accused were the culprits and had to be punished for their mistreatment of their grandmother. But I've come to realize that the bond between a mother and a child is so beautiful, so sacred, and infinite that despite of whatever wrong a child does to a mother, she still tries to protect them. As is the case with Mrs. Earl. For, your honor, she would prefer to stay with her grandchildren, whatever the circumstances be, than stay apart from them or make them suffer for their ill doings. I think if she can forgive these two, then perhaps so can the justice system.

JUDGE

I see.

MELISSA

Although, I would request to the state that they ensure the Social Worker be allowed to make welfare visitations once Mrs. Earl is released from the care home. And also give updates on her progress.

The Social Worker smiles and nods, happy with the prosecutor's decision.

JUDGE

In light of the recommendations, the
court has decided to release Mrs. Earl
back to the care of her grandchildren.
All charges against them are being
dropped, and the state also directs
the Social Worker to make welfare
visitations on Mrs. Earl regularly.
The court is adjourned.

The judge strikes the gavel, and the camera
zooms in on it.

Freeze

ACT IX

Scene 1

Ext-Street-Day

The camera opens with a van coming to a halt outside the house 4801. The camera tracks as an orderly steps out from the front and goes to the back of the van to take Mrs. Earl's wheelchair out. A squad car also parks behind them, and a deputy and Tyler and Emma step out of the car.

The camera then pans from them to across the street, where the neighbors have come out in their front yard to watch this scene.

                    SHEILA

     Good God, they've brought Mrs. Earl
     back to live with them.

                    THOMAS

     What a travesty! I don't like this.

The camera tracks from their POV as Mrs. Earl and the teenagers are escorted into the house. Then, the camera pans back to them.

                    THOMAS

     I don't understand why they would send
     her back to live with such horrible
     grandchildren. Hadn't they done enough
     damage?

SHEILA

God knows… but let's just hope that this time around, they've learned their lesson and are good to her.

THOMAS

I highly doubt that, but let's pray nevertheless.

Cut

Scene 2

Int-bedroom-evening

The camera opens in the dimly lit bedroom. It pans on Mrs. Earl who's lying awake, taking in her surroundings. She seems to be in good health. She looks at the photos on the wall and smiles. The room's door opens with a thud, and a drunken Tyler swaggers in.

TYLER

You've caused us a lot of trouble, old woman… I was friggin' sent to jail because of ya, and poor Emma had to rot in juvie… I wish I could do something to you, but that bloody prosecutor has put that Social Worker on our case again, and it's all cuz of ya.

The grandmother looks at him with fear in her eyes as Tyler menacingly threatens her. Her lips quiver with fear as Tyler slowly moves toward her and shakes her shoulders angrily.

TYLER

Why the hell are you still a pain in our ass….

EMMA

Stop it Ty… stop it… you're gonna kill her. Leave her alone!

Emma drags him away from the old woman, who is sobbing by now. Emma then forcefully pushes Tyler out of the room and shuts it behind her as she also leaves. The camera stops on the closed door.

Scene 3

Int-lounge-day

Tyler is smoking pot, listening to some music, and lying on the couch. Emma is munching on the chips and reading a magazine. Suddenly, they hear the sound of breaking glass, and they both flinch.

TYLER

Not this shit again, man… go see what she has done now.

Emma gets up from the couch and makes a face. The camera tracks her as she makes her way toward her grandmother's room.

Cut

Scene 3-A

Int-bedroom-day

The camera opens in the middle of the room
and tracks to the shards of broken glass
and water spilled on the floor. Then tracks
to Mrs. Earl half in and half out of the
bed. It clearly seems she was trying to
help herself to the glass of water.

As Emma walks near her and helps her get
back in bed, a disgusted look on her face.
The old woman sobs.

                    MRS. EARL

        Wwww…aaa…ter

Emma says nothing and simply goes out of
the room and comes back with a glass of
water and hands it to the old woman who can
barely hold the glass as her hands are
shaking from weakness, and she spills some
water.

                    EMMA

        For heaven's sake

Emma angrily takes the glass back and
roughly helps the grandmother drink the
water, some of the water spilling on her
clothes. Emma then puts the glass back and
gives the woman a withering look.

                    EMMA

        You do realize that you're still

nothing but a damn burden. Why couldn't it have been you instead of Mama?

Emma sneers as she starts sweeping the floor. The camera pans back to the old woman who's silently weeping.

Cut

Scene 4

Ext-Porch-Day

The Social Worker nervously knocks on the door, fidgeting with her purse straps. She takes a step back when the door is abruptly opened, and Tyler comes into view.

                    TYLER

What the hell ya doin' here?

                SOCIAL WORKER

Hello… I am here for the court-ordered visit.

                    TYLER

I see… please come in.

Tyler made space for her and gestured her inside. The Social Worker took a sigh of relief and stepped past him. Tyler looks at the street and then quickly shuts the door. He then grabs the Social Worker by the elbow, startling her.

                    SOCIAL WORKER

Wh.. what the hell do you think you're
doing?

                    TYLER

Now listen! You've been a real bitch
and a pain in my ass, and this time
around, I'm not gonna let you snitch,
so you better believe if you go around
saying anything about us to the
police, I'm gonna make you pay. I know
how to find you. So, you and your
family can be touched; don't ever
forget!

                    SOCIAL WORKER

You can't threaten me like that.

                    TYLER

Oh really? Wanna try me?

The Social Worker looks at him with a
horrified expression.

                    SOCIAL WORKER

This is extortion.

                    TYLER

Call it what you want, but fuck with
us again, and you're screwed. Now go
check on ma grandma and get the hell
out of here.

The Social Worker quickly rushes out of the lounge.

Fade Out

Scene 5

Int-Bedroom-Day

The Social Worker opens the room's door and quickly covers her nose due to the smell permeating in the air. She ventures in and sees that the old woman is lying in tangled sheets, her face once again haggard, and the sheets she's lying on are soiled. The Social Worker quickly checks on the woman, and a tear escapes her eyes.

                    SOCIAL WORKER

        Oh, Mrs. Earl, why did you choose this
        hell for you again?

Just then, Emma enters the room, and the woman turns around and gives Emma a disgusted and disappointed look. Emma looks at her and then looks away.

Cut

Scene 6

Int-Hospital room-Day

The camera opens into a maternity ward and tracks to a private room. Melissa is sitting on a hospital bed with a newborn child cradled in her arms. She smiles at

the child as she lovingly places a soft
kiss on the baby's forehead.

Cut

Scene: Montage

- Melissa is busy in her new life,
  taking care of the baby, and is shown
  playing with the baby in her nursery.

- Mrs. Earl's health is deteriorating,
  and she looks haggard. She is lying
  against the cushions and having a
  coughing fit. As she recovers, the
  camera zooms in on the blood trickling
  from the side of her mouth.

- Tyler is having a party in his
  backyard with his friends, smoking
  weed and drinking.

- The Social Worker is in a playground,
  watching her kids. She looks to the
  other side and watches Tyler grinning
  at her. He looks at her and puts a
  finger on his lips, motioning her to
  remain silent.

- The Social Worker is in her office and
  is writing a report and signs all
  clear on it while wiping away a tear.

Fade Out.

Scene 8

Int-Bedroom-Night

The camera opens in the room and tracks slowly toward the bed, and the figure lying in the middle of it wrapped in sheets. The sheets are stained with blood and fecal matter. The camera zooms in on the old woman taking labored breaths, a photo frame of her husband and her daughter is clutched to her chest as tears pour down her face. The woman starts choking, and it's obvious she's in the throes of death. Suddenly, her body spasms, and then she takes one last breath. A contented smile on her face before her face goes lax and the photo frame clutched to her chest clatters to the floor. The camera zooms in on the cracked glass of the frame.

Freeze

Act X

Scene 1:

Int-Kitchen-Night

The camera opens into the dinghy kitchen, panning from grimy walls to Emma making dinner and singing to herself. She looks in a good mood and is swaying to the song she is singing.

                    O/L

     Loud crash

Emma's hands are still, and she stops singing. She quickly switches off the stove and groans.

                    EMMA
     The fuck, has she broken now…

She quickly rushes out of the kitchen, and the camera tracks her as she passes the corridor leading to her grandmother's room. Angrily, she pushes open the door.

                              Cut to

Scene 2:

Int-Bedroom-Night

The room door bangs open, and the camera zooms in on Emma's thunderous expressions.

                    EMMA

       What the hell hav…

The camera focuses on her changing
expressions, from anger to horror, as her
eyes go wide. The camera pans from her to
the shattered frame lying on the floor.
Shards of glass glistening as the camera
tracks them toward the bed where the old
woman is lying, her face lax and gray. Emma
slowly walks toward the bed.

                    EMMA

       Grandma… Grandma…

She calls out, sidestepping the broken frame
and looking at her dead grandmother. The
camera zooms in on the old woman, her mouth
agape, drool crusting near her lips, and tear
tracks on her wrinkled face. Emma, not
believing what she's seeing, tentatively
shakes the old woman's shoulders but finds no
movement. She again calls her out.

                    EMMA

       Grandma, c'mon, open your eyes.

Emma looks on the verge of tears, and a
gasp breaks free, realizing what has
happened. She takes a step back, and her
feet crunch on the shards of broken glass.
She looks down and notices the picture in
the frame. She picks up the frame, and it's
a picture of her mother alongside her

parents, all of them beaming at the camera. The camera zooms in on the picture.

Cut

Scene 3:

Int-Nursery-Night

The camera opens in a bedroom converted into a nursery. The camera tracks to Melissa sitting on a rocking chair and singing a lullaby to a child.

MELISSA

Arrorro Mi Nino…

Melissa looks tenderly at her baby and smiles.

Cut

Scene 4:

Int-Bedroom-Night

The camera tracks to Emma sitting on the floor against the bed, her head buried and her arms around her legs. Her sobs grow louder, and suddenly, the room door crashes open.

TYLER

What the fuck is wrong?

                    EMMA

    looks up and gives him a look of
    loathing, and says nothing. Tyler
    gives her a confused look, then, out
    of some instinct, moves toward the
    bed. He sees the dead figure, the old
    woman, and quickly steps back.

                    TYLER

    The fuck...

The camera zooms in on his horrified
expressions, panning back to the motionless
figure of the old woman.

                                        Cut

Scene 5

Int-Lounge-Night

                    THOMAS

    They killed her... I told you they
    would... the state made a horrible
    mistake.

Sheila stood up from the couch as a
harried-looking Thomas entered the lounge.
The camera swivels from his agitated
expressions to Sheila's horrified ones.

                    SHEILA

    Is Mrs. Earl...

THOMAS

Dead… I just saw the ambulance pull up
and her being wheeled out of the
house.

SHEILA

Maybe you're mistaken. What if it's
just a health scare like previous
times.

THOMAS

I'm not mistaken. I heard the
paramedics; they declared her dead and
talked about police showing up any
minute.

SHEILA

Oh, honey. Poor Mrs. Earl, but at
least she no longer has to live with
those monsters. Finally, she's free.

Thomas nods, a grim expression on his face.

Cut

Scene 6:

Ext-Street-Night

The paramedics are zipping up the body bag
containing Mrs. Earl as they wheel her
inside the ambulance. The camera pans from
them to Tyler and Emma being walked out in
handcuffs. Tyler is fighting his arrest,

whereas Emma looks defeated, a lost expression on her face as they are both pushed inside the squad cars and taken away. The camera tracks to the closed door of house 4801.

Cut

Scene 7-A

Int-Office-Day

The Social Worker is sitting in her office, discussing a case file with a colleague. The camera pans the small, cramped room, tracking to the desk covered with files and papers.

COLLEAGUE

I'll email you the rest of the details. Meanwhile, kindly make a visit as soon as possible.

The Social Worker nods, and the colleague exits. The phone rings, and she picks it up.

SOCIAL WORKER

Hello… are you sure? (pause) I see. Thank you for informing.

With trembling fingers, she puts the phone back on the cradle, and a sob escapes her. The camera zooms in on her as she starts weeping.

Cut

Scene 7-B

Int-Lounge-Day

The camera opens into a brightly lit room, tracking from the entryway to the floor littered with toys. A six-month-old baby is lying on the carpeted floor, playing with a teddy bear. Melissa is sitting next to him, making baby noises as the baby laughs. The camera pans toward her cell phone as it starts ringing.

MELISSA

Hello

SOCIAL WORKER

Melissa… It's me… remember Mrs. Earl, the old lady whose grandchildren mistreated her… she… she died… the kids have been arrested.

MELISSA

Oh… I…uh, thank you for letting me know. Goodbye.

Melissa ends the call and looks at her child. She smiles as her baby makes funny noises. She looks at the baby intently, the camera tracking her movements as a tear slips her eye before her smile turns into a sob.

MELISSA

Ohhhh Mrs. Earl

She looks outside the window at the sky,
and the camera tracks from her to the sky
through the window.

                                        Freeze.

                        The End